MY BODY'S

POWER PACK

HOW TO MANAGE YOUR ENERGY and STAY IN CHARGE!

Sandhya Menon

Illustrated by Kushla Ross

Jessica Kingsley Publishers

London and Philadelphia

To all the neurodivergent children and
adults who are learning to make space
for their bodies' needs, this book is for you.

First published in Great Britain in 2025 by Jessica Kingsley Publishers

An imprint of John Murray Press

1

Copyright © Sandhya Menon 2025

The right of Sandhya Menon to be identified as the Author of the Work has been asserted by them in accordance with the Copyright, Designs and Patents Act 1988.

Front cover image source: Kushla Ross.

A CIP catalogue record for this title is available from the British Library and the Library of Congress

ISBN 978 1 80501 825 4

eISBN 978 1 80501 826 1

Printed and bound in China by Leo Paper Products Ltd

Jessica Kingsley Publishers' policy is to use papers that are natural, renewable and recyclable products and made from wood grown in sustainable forests. The logging and manufacturing processes are expected to conform to the environmental regulations of the country of origin.

Jessica Kingsley Publishers
Carmelite House
50 Victoria Embankment
London EC4Y 0DZ

www.jkp.com

John Murray Press
Part of Hodder & Stoughton Ltd
An Hachette Company

The authorised representative in the EEA is Hachette Ireland,
8 Castlecourt Centre, Dublin 15, D15 XTP3, Ireland (email: info@hbgi.ie)

Power packs can...

RUMBLE and

FEELING: WORRIED   35% CHARGE SOON

SWOOSH!

and

ENERGETIC   80% FAST CHARGE
FEELING: ENERGETIC

and

CRASH

ROAR

GOOD   95% ALMOST CHARGED
FEELING: GOOD

13% LOW CHARGE
FEELING: LOW

My body does all of that
and so much more.

My power pack stores my energy.
It goes up and down each day.

Some days are high, others low.
Sometimes, they're just okay.

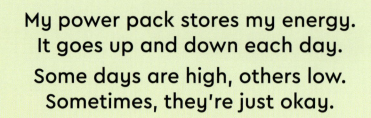

When my power pack is full,
my body is ready to go.

3, 2, 1 LIFT OFF!
Oh, I feel all aglow.

When I'm on full charge,
my days are happy and bright.
Going through the day is easier
when everything feels just right.

FEELING:
HAPPY 😁

100%

FULL CHARGE

My body wants to move and groove, to run and dance around!

FEELING:
JOYFUL 😄

100%

FULL CHARGE

Joy flows from the top of my head to my toes down on the ground.

But it doesn't last forever.
There are days I lose my charge.
It's those sneaky Drainer Gremlins
with green toes and ears so large.

Watch now – here the Dremlins come!
Tiptoe, tiptoe, tiptoe.
They unplug my power pack's charger
and watch it get LOW, LOW, LOW.

LOW CHARGE

FEELING: TIRED 😐   38% CHARGE SOON

The Drainer Gremlins love
the chaos when things go wrong.
When I'm unwell or sad or
sing the wrong note in a song.

They come when I'm unsure
of how to start or what to do.
When the teacher doesn't pick
me, and instead, they pick you.

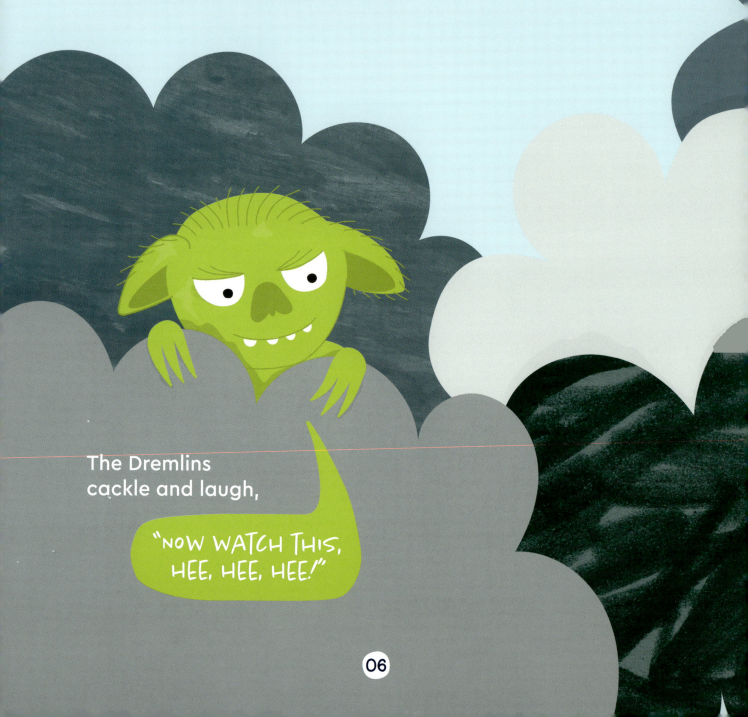

The Dremlins
cackle and laugh,

"NOW WATCH THIS,
HEE, HEE, HEE!"

I don't feel so good anymore,
my energy's trickled down.
I feel the shift in my body,
but you only see a tiny frown.

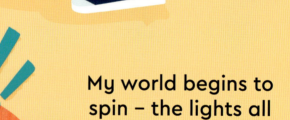

My world begins to spin – the lights all

FLICKER
and
FLASH

Noises merge –
**ONE
ON
TOP**
of the other.

I'm no longer in control without power in my pack.
My body takes over; it might shut down,
run away or attack.

The Dremlins come when life gets tricky.
That's when my power starts to fall.
But I know who I am at my lowest
is just part of me, not all.

Sometimes, it's hard to speak or
smile when I'm feeling down.
It helps when someone safe is there,
who I can be all of myself around.

We all have unique power
packs that, over time,
we get to know.

Some power packs drain fast,
while other packs drain slow.

FEELING:
EXHAUSTED
20%
LOW
CHARGE

FEELING:
CURIOUS
88%
HIGH
CHARGE

FEELING:
PROUD ☺
92%
ALMOST
FULL
CHARGE

FEELING:
NERVOUS
54%
CHARGE
LOWERING

QUIET

the
BIG
DOOR

With some help, I can work out
which charger is just right for me.

I wonder and I wonder... what could
my special boost of energy be?

Could it be unicorns galloping
along or dragons flying high?

Perhaps it's building blocks
or spotting planes in the sky.

TRICKLE, TRICKLE, TRIC-
a break brings energy back.

20%

FEELING: SLEEPY 😊 NOW CHARGING

45%

FEELING: CONTENT 😊 NOW CHARGING

Quiet spaces,
lots of cuddles;
perhaps I'll have
a snack.

PLIP, PLIP, PLOP–

I'm on my way back. →

GLOOP, GLOOP, GLOOP–

with a charged-up power pack.

19

Those pesky Drainer Gremlins!
Some are here to stay.

Try as I might, things will pop up –
they won't always go my way.

But I'm working it all out – when they come and where.
My deep power lies in knowing and being aware.

So, HA HA, watch now, Dremlins;
you can't get the best of me!
You can drain me, but I'll charge back up.
Knowing what I need is key.

Sometimes,
I need peace and
quiet after different
types of sound.

Other times, I might
need lots of space
to dance and
move around.

There are days when I need help working out the rules of play.

Often, I need time to think when there are changes to the day.

DIARY

TODAY

1 MATHS
2 PE
3 ART
4 ~~LIBRARY~~

FORGOT BOOKS☹

I can wear my trusty headphones.
I can ask when I don't understand.

Sometimes, I'll play by myself,
lining up rocks in the sand.

I'll share my uncomfortable feelings
when those Dremlins start to come.
I'll find my safe people to get help from
– maybe teachers, friends, Dad or Mum.

FEELING: RELAXED 😌

60% ALMOST FULL

Those hard days are getting easier.
I know my chargers now, you see.
I know my power pack well,
and I'm in charge of me.

These ups and downs are part of life; avoiding them is not the goal. With a little bit of support and love, yes,

I'M TAKING BACK CONTROL!

FEELING: CONFIDENT

99%

CHARGING NOW

ABOUT *the* AUTHOR

Sandhya Menon is a neurodivergent author, professional speaker and psychologist residing on Wurundjeri Land in Naarm, otherwise known as Melbourne in Australia. Her other children's books include *The Brain Forest*, which introduces neurodiversity as a concept, and *The Rainbow Brain*, which is the first book of its kind to describe what it's like to be both autistic and an ADHDer.

In her role as a psychologist, Sandhya saw the need for clearer emotional regulation strategies that dealt with the root causes of big feelings. She created the *What's Up Flip Chart* in 2021 as a visual tool to help children communicate their emotions and needs to an adult. Over the years, in clinical practice, she continued to expand her understanding of emotional regulation work based on nervous system distress, regulation abilities and unmet needs. And from there, this book, *My Body's Power Pack*, was born.

Energy accounting is part of Sandhya's everyday life, through managing herself and supporting young children. She uses biotrackers to understand her body's energy and stress markers better, and is amazed at how much she is learning about neurodivergent responses to everyday stress.

Sandhya can often be found in a dark, quiet room after social events, grateful for a partner who recognizes the need for deep rest. She is still learning how to recognize, meet and advocate for her needs across different contexts, and is a constant work in progress.

AUTHOR'S NOTE

Energy accounting is a philosophy that applies to all humans, as it speaks to our nervous systems. I hope the concepts of drainers and chargers help you to understand your own needs and power pack so you, too, can work out how to balance everyday life and routines sustainably. I look forward to hearing from you about how life changes when you give yourself permission to meet your needs unashamedly.

To the neurodivergent readers, here's to gently giving ourselves permission to examine and question neuro-normative expectations and move away from them where possible. Here's to celebrating you doing you, living life boldly.

Yours,
Sandhya Menon

Resources

This book was inspired by Spoon Theory, created by Christine Miserandino. While initially designed to talk about the energy limitations that can come with lupus, a chronic illness, this theory has proven helpful for many different cross-sections of the neurodivergent population. *My Body's Power Pack* expands on this theory using the metaphor of a battery to increase its relatability amongst children.

My Body's Power Pack can be an alternative to traditional emotional regulation and anger management strategies, and is based on a deep neurobiological understanding of how nervous systems operate. This perspective highlights how a build-up of stress can lead to a meltdown or shutdown, rather than looking at emotions purely on a cause-and-effect level. This lens helps us zoom out and examine behaviours within the larger context, putting in place holistic strategies that truly support individuals.

Here are a few ways that parents, carers, clinicians and educators can use this resource:

To foster inclusion and understanding

Every human has a nervous system, so it follows that everyone has a power pack. In a classroom, this can spark conversation about how different students have different drainers and, therefore, need more or less time to charge.

For example, it's easy for some people to sit on the mat, so it is not a big drainer. Other students may find it physically painful to sit still for long periods, and, therefore, the same activity can be a big drainer.

A teacher can ask students about the size of their Drainer Gremlins in different situations and brainstorm ideas on how to keep the "Dremlin" at bay. Students may chime in with ideas and discussions, leading to the normalization of different needs in a classroom. This method is student-led, collaborative and inclusive, which goes a long way toward fostering understanding and acceptance among peers.

To help neurodivergent people meet their own needs

Parents, carers, clinicians and educators can use this resource to help explain fight-or-flight scenarios and why some children may have meltdowns. The power pack language offers a way to build awareness of their drainers in a non-stigmatizing way and supports them to be compassionate about and understanding of their needs in context. This can help shift the language from "angry/naughty/bad child" to "I had too many drainers today", inviting self-compassion. Whilst primarily using an autistic lens in this book, these concepts can be personalized across a wide cross-section of the population.

Looking to put this into practice?

Check out this book's accompanying resource pack, other books and resources here:

FOR OTHER BOOKS AND RESOURCES

www.onwardsandupwardspsychology.com.au/shop-1

OF RELATED INTEREST

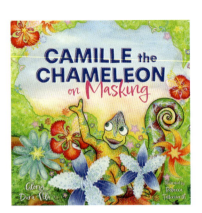

Camille the Chameleon on Masking
How to Stop Masking and Discover your Awesome Autistic Self

Gloria Dura-Vila
Illustrated by Rebecca Tatternorth
ISBN 978 1 80501 103 3
eISBN 978 1 80501 104 0

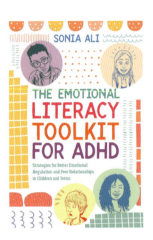

The Emotional Literacy Toolkit for ADHD
Strategies for Better Emotional Regulation and Peer Relationships in Children and Teens

Sonia Ali
ISBN 978 1 83997 426 7
eISBN 978 1 83997 427 4

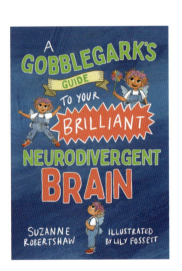

A Gobblegark's Guide to Your Brilliant Neurodivergent Brain

Suzanne Robertshaw
Illustrated by Lily Fossett
ISBN 978 1 83997 852 4
eISBN 978 1 83997 853 1